102 REASONS TO BELIEVE IN JESUS AND TO SERVE HIM ONLY

IVAN BLAKE

ISBN 978-1-0980-8609-1 (paperback)
ISBN 978-1-0980-8610-7 (digital)

Christian Faith Publishing
832 Park Avenue
Meadville, PA 16335
www.christianfaithpublishing.com

Printed in the United States of America

1. The mystery of the birth of Jesus Christ by a virgin is still unreal to some people, even beyond the mystery of the birth of Jesus. Do you accept Him (Jesus) as God with you? It is so comforting and peaceful to know you always have your God with you.

2. If the blind walks with the blind, they will stumble. If the fool walks with the fool, they will lose their way. If the wise walks with the wise, they will do great exploits. The three wise men traveled from the east to Bethlehem of Judah. They travelled an estimated 9,125 miles for two and a half years at ten miles a day to worship Jesus and to be the reckoned with the wise.

3. Sickness and infirmities are great problems to both men and beasts. Thank the Lord Jesus for good doctors who try to help us when we are sick, but they will not (and cannot) bear our sicknesses and infirmities for us. But Jesus took our infirmities and bore them in his own body when He (Jesus) died on Calvary's cross. Jesus tasted death for every man—even you.

4. Have you ever seen a great storm on land? How terrifying is it? Have you ever experienced a storm in the sea? How terrible is it? I am so glad I have Jesus with me to still the terrible storms of life when they are raging around me. When the storms of life are raging about you, who do you have in your life to still the storms?

You too can have Jesus if you want Him. Do you want Him? Yes or no?

5. How bad is it to be sick with an incurable disease? But how wonderful is it to have good friends to help in times of sickness? However, they can't do much more. How wonderful it is to know that Jesus knows us and knows our deepest needs. He saw a sick man and his friends and stepped in and healed him, and forgave him of his sins. He can do the same for you. If you are a sinner, Jesus is your savior.

6. There are many things that men can do upon the earth, with the exception of forgiving sins. How surprising to the Pharisees and others to hear Jesus saying to the sick man, "Thy sins are forgiven." Do you know that only Jesus can forgive you of your sins? Why not go to Him today if you know that Jesus has power on earth to forgive you of your sins?

7. All leaders in any organization seek impeccable or holier-than-thou persons to follow them. Those who lead must have a good record and must be well recommended by others. Our God, the holy one of Israel, the Lord Jesus, came not to call the righteous but sinners to repentance. Don't let your bad record define you. Jesus wants to save you.

8. Joseph interpreted the dreams of the servants of the king of Egypt when they were all in prison. The servants were released from prison, as Joseph interpreted, and exactly what Joseph predicted would happen to them happened. When they returned to the king, they forgot Joseph and did not mention his name. But if any man confesses the name of Jesus before his Father, who is in heaven, Jesus will not forget your name. Confess Him, and confess Him now.

9. Do you love Jesus more than your mother and your father or sons and daughters? If you do, you will do well. If you don't, you are not worthy of His (Jesus's) love! Is there anything in your life that you love more than Jesus? Yes or no?

10. When John was in prison and was about to die, he was so discouraged; he was not certain if Jesus was the savior who should come into the world. He sent his disciples to ask Jesus if He was the one who would come into the world as the savior. Jesus replied to John's disciples, "Go and tell John the things you have seen and heard." John had comfort in prison and in death because he was assured who Jesus is. What do you see, and what do you hear? Are you sure who Jesus is in your life? Can you die with the assurance of who Jesus is? Yes or no?

11. When Israel was enslaved in Egypt, they served the Egyptians with rigor and their burden was heavy. But when Jesus, the great deliverer, delivered Israel out of Egypt and took them into the land of Canaan, the Lord gave Israel rest from their labour. Labour is made rest and burdens are light when Jesus is near, for Jesus carries your heavy burdens and carries your heavy load when you let Him.

12. A good name means much. Proverbs 22:1 says, "A good name is rather to be chosen than great riches." The Gentiles, who were not God's people, trusted in the name of Jesus and became God's people. Do you trust in Jesus's name? I do.

13. Who do you call to when your life begins to sink? Whose hand will you hold on to when your life is in great despair? Seek a friend before you need one. Jesus is a friend you can call on anytime. Precious Lord, take my hand.

14. What a great business deal it is to work for Jesus. There is hardly any business that can yield you 100 percent fold. But in whatever you do for Jesus, you are guaranteed 100 percent plus eternal life. Will you work for Jesus now? It pays 100 percent fold and endless days; what a great reward! Do you want Jesus? Yes or no?

15. Many adults refuse to serve the Lord Jesus as their maker and savior. If you should ask them why they refuse to serve the Lord, some will say they are not ready yet. Like the scribes, the Pharisees, and the Sadducees, they were annoyed at Jesus and chided Him over what the children were saying. I can hear Jesus saying "Oh, what a gracious praise coming out of the mouth of the babe and suckling." Jesus called it perfect. Can you give Jesus a perfect praise as the children did? Yes or no?

16. The name of Jesus brings an holy hatred by the world. The apostles were warned not to preach or teach in the name of Jesus. Stephen was stoned to death for the name. Peter, James, and John were put in jail for the name of Jesus. They were mocked and hated for the name of Jesus. Are you hated for the name of Jesus, or do you hate the name of Jesus?

17. When the Lord shall send his angels to gather together his elect from the four winds, from one end of the heaven to the other, will you be in the gathering or will you be left behind? I want to be in the number. I will be in the number when the trumpet sounds. I want to see the Son of Man when He comes in the cloud of the heaven with great power and glory.

18. How great is the Word of Jesus to you? Do you love His words? Do you obey His words? Do you read His words? Do you understand His words? When all things shall pass away, the Word of Jesus shall stand.

19. When all nations shall be gathered together by the Lord Jesus and when He shall separate the nations as a good shepherd separates the sheep from the goats, which side will you be on? Sheep or goat?

20. The shed blood of Jesus brings in a new and living way; it erases the old way and the old things. The blood of Jesus was shed for the remission of sins. Though your sins be as scarlet, Jesus will wash them white as snow. Are you washed in Jesus's blood? If not, you can be, if you are willing to be cleansed from your sins and your old ways.

21–

22. Jesus, the true God of all power, has sent His disciples to go into the entire world to teach them who Jesus is and what they should do to be saved. Those who believe should be baptized in the name of the Father, the Son, and the Holy Ghost. What is the name of the Father, the Son, and the Holy Ghost? Jesus!

23. I know something that the Lord doesn't know; I know someone who is greater than I am. Jesus does not know anyone who is greater than He is. John said of Jesus that he, John, was "not worthy to stoop and unloose the latchets of Jesus's shoes." John the Baptist was the first to baptize people in water. Jesus spoke of John the Baptist, saying, "Of all the prophets who was born of a woman, there arise no greater prophet." But John showed greater reverence to Jesus as the one who will baptize with the Holy Ghost. Are you willing to be baptized in water, in the name of Jesus, so that Jesus will baptize you with the Holy Ghost? Yes or no?

24. Will you join in the search to find Jesus? As the people who found Him said, "all men seeketh for thee." Are

you seeking for Jesus? And better yet, have you found Him? Yes or no?

25. When you know Jesus as the one and only true God, then you will understand that He alone can forgive you of your sins. Do you know that Jesus is the way? Yes or no?

26. There are some great people who have done great things that have caused us to wonder: things in building construction, aircraft, medicine, sports, and the list goes on. But do you wonder about the great things that Jesus has done and the things Jesus is still doing? When Jesus stilled the wind and the waves, the disciples asked in astonishment, "What manner of man is this, that even the winds and the waves obey Him!" The sea saw Him and fled, the dead fish heard Him and multiplied, and the water heard Him and turned into wine. What has Jesus done in your life that causes you to wonder?

27. The statement "Be of good cheer" is said to be in the Bible 365 times, one time for each day of the year. With each occurrence, God is reminding us "I am God, and I am able to supply all your needs." There is no trouble, trial, sorrow, or grief that Jesus cannot see you through. We do not have to be afraid when we know that Jesus is with us. If you call upon Jesus in faith, believing, He will help you.

28. You may not have a village, city, or country for Jesus to enter, but if you open your heart's door to Jesus, He will enter in and make you whole. Try it now.

29. It is said that of the 7.53 billion people in the world today, only 7 percent are geniuses. Furthermore, only 1 percent of geniuses will accomplish the things they started out to do exactly as they wanted it to be. But Jesus does all things well. He made the heavens and the earth, the sea, and all that is in them exactly how He

wanted: perfect. Who will you depend on to do what you want done? Jesus, who does all things well, or the genius who will fail?

30. When Jesus asked His disciples, "Whom do men say that I the Son of Man am?" the disciples gave to Jesus the opinion of the public, saying, "Some say that thou art John the Baptist: some, Elias; and others, one of the prophets." Jesus gave His disciples their first test by asking them their personal opinion of Him. Peter answered, saying, "Thou art the Christ." I pose a personal question for you today: who do you say Jesus is to you? A good man or God in the flesh?

31. There are some parents who are ashamed of their children, and there are some children who are ashamed of their parents. There are servants who are ashamed of their masters and masters ashamed of their servants, and the list goes on and on. Who are you ashamed of? Are you in the number that is ashamed of Jesus, or do you embrace Jesus? Don't wait until you see Jesus in His glory to embrace Him. Jesus will be ashamed of you on that day.

32. All men desire to be ministered to and seek for their own. But the Son of Man (Jesus) came to minister to every man and to give His life for all. Will you allow Jesus to minister to you and save you?

33. When a king, president, prime minister, or any other dignitary travels to a country, city, or town, they travel with an entourage to discourage the common people from getting too close to them. When Jesus went through the cities, He had no security and no important person with Him announcing His coming. The common people ran to Him, some before Him and some behind Him, shouting the highest praise to Jesus, say-

ing, "Hosanna; Blessed is he that cometh in the name of the Lord." Which crowd will you be in? The crowd for Jesus or the crowd of the world?

34. What do you make of the Lord's house? Do you take it for a den of thieves or a holy place of worship? The Word of God says in Psalm 93:5, "Holiness becometh thy house, oh Lord." Psalm 26:8 says, "Lord, I have loved the habitation of thy house, and the place where thine honor dwelleth." Do you love the house of the Lord?

35. The words "I Am," concerning the Lord Jesus, is found in the King James Bible 973 times. It was first mentioned in Genesis 15:1, and the last time in Revelation 22:16. It was first spoken by the Lord to Abraham and for the last time to John by Jesus. The quote means everything that Jesus is. Who is the "I Am" to you? Jesus, the I Am, is everything to me. He is my all in all. What about you?

36. Jesus was rejected as the king of Israel and the king of the Jews by the Pharisees and the scribes. Is Jesus your king? Do you worship Him or are you straying away from Him? Are you crucifying Him as the crowd at Calvary did? Remember that Jesus is the King of kings. He is also the King of glory, the King of peace, the King of immortality, and the King eternal. Someway, sometime, you will have to acknowledge Him (Jesus) as your king.

37. Are these signs following you? If they are, you are a believer. If not, you need to become a believer, and these signs shall follow you. Yes, for "greater is He (Jesus) that is in you than he that is in the world."

38. The accolades of Jesus are so great. Who would not want to be with Him? He was named by an angel and

not a man. Before He was born, greatness was pro-
nounced upon Him. He is the son of the highest. He
shall reign over the throne of His father, David. Who
was the greatest king of Israel? David reigned over Israel
for forty years. Jesus reigns over the heaven and earth
forever. The Bible says of His kingdom there shall be no
end. Are you a subject of His, or are you a stranger to
His kingdom?

39.   Good news is very hard to come by, so people say no
news is good news. But the angels of the Lord said,
"Behold, I bring you good tidings of great joy, which
shall be to all people." There are tidings that are not for
everyone, but the tidings of the birth of Jesus are good
tidings; it is great joy, and it is for everyone.

40.   Simeon's joy was fulfilled when he saw Jesus that he
requested to die. David declared in Psalms, "I shall not
die but live to declare the works of the Lord." When you
think about seeing Jesus, the great God of the universe,
you think, what else is left for you to see? Jesus is the
light that lightens every man who comes into the world.
He (Jesus) is the light that lights the Gentiles. He is the
glory of Israel. If your heart can conceive Him and your
eyes can ever behold Him, maybe you would ask the
same request of Simeon, for what greater person is there
to see when I see Jesus? Amen.

41.   Of the six things that is in Luke 4:18–19, Jesus came to
do what appeals to every man. The poor have the gospel
preached to them. The gospel is the only thing that the
poor have equal with the rich. Sometimes, somehow,
we have a broken heart, and almost all of us are taken
captive by something. Furthermore, all of us who are
born of a woman are taken captive by sin. Our only
way of escape is by what Jesus has done for us all. Every

one of us is born spiritually blind, and some of us are physically blind. Either way, Jesus came to give us sight. We are all battered and bruised by life's problems, trying to free ourselves but can't. Jesus came to set us free. Whom the Son sets free is free indeed. Luke 4:19 is the game changer; Jesus came to preach the acceptable year of the Lord.

42. It is heartrending to know that demons know who Jesus is but men, of whom are made in the likeness of and image of God, don't know who Jesus is. Do you know who Jesus is? Are you welcoming Jesus, or are you saying, like the demons, "Leave us alone"?

43. The Lord Jesus is known to do things immediately. Just as He put forth His hand and touched the leper, the leper was cleansed. Jesus immediately turned the water into wine. Jesus touched the eyes of the blind, and they immediately saw. What do you want Jesus to do for you? Say it out loud, believe it, and Jesus will do it now.

44. Can you hear Jesus calling your name? Will you follow His command? Jesus said to Simon Peter, "Follow me," and Peter straightway left his boat and followed Jesus. Jesus said to Levi, "Follow me," and Levi immediately left the seat of customs and followed Jesus. What will you give up to follow Jesus? Only what you do for Jesus will last.

45. One of the great contentions of the Bible is centered around the Sabbath day. The scribes and Pharisees always questioned Jesus and His disciples about the Sabbath day; they always accused Jesus of breaking the Sabbath. Jesus answered and said unto them that He (Jesus) is the Lord of the Sabbath. The word *Lord* means "owner" or "maker." Is Jesus your maker? The word of

David in the Psalms says, "It is He that made us." My maker is my Lord, even Jesus.

46. How much can a touch do, anyway? Ask the people of Jesus's day: those who were sick in anywise or had any broken or withered limbs who sought to touch Jesus. Everyone was healed of their sicknesses because virtue went out from Him (Jesus) and healed them all.

47. Love is not love until you give it away. When you give it away, it will come back to you. If you try to save it, you will lose it. But if you give your life to Jesus and lose your life for Christ's sake, you will find life again.

48. Have you ever heard Jesus's voice? His voice makes the difference. The wind and the water heard His voice, obeyed Him, and became still. Jesus spoke to the deaf, and they heard Him. Though Lazarus was dead, Jesus called him, and he came forth. Jesus's voice makes the difference. Have you ever heard Jesus calling your name?

49. The rulers of this world are making weapons of mass destruction for no reason at all other than to destroy men's lives. Jesus, who made us, came into the world not to destroy men's lives but to save us. Are you saved? Do you want to be saved? If you are not saved, ask Jesus to save you. Jesus is willing and able to save you. None who come to Jesus will be cast away.

50. What a name! What a powerful name! What an excellent name! The name of Jesus! The name of Jesus is so great, even devils are made subject to the disciples of Jesus when they call upon the name of Jesus. Are you calling upon the lovely name of Jesus?

51. When Jesus walked the shores of Galilee, His true identity was a mystery to most people. Some said He was a carpenter's son. Some said He was a wine bibber. Others said He was Elias or one of the prophets. You cannot

guess who Jesus is. For you to truly know who He is, Jesus will have to reveal himself to you. Jesus revealed himself to the woman at the well when He (Jesus) said, "I am he that speaks." He spoke to Mary at His resurrection. Jesus said unto her, "I am He." He also spoke to Saul on the road to Damascus. Saul asked, "Who art thou, Lord?" The Lord answered him and said, "I am Jesus." Ask for Jesus, and He will reveal himself to you. When you know Him, you will serve Him.

52–

53. Solomon was known to be the wisest man of all time. The Lord gave unto Solomon special wisdom above all men. All the rulers of his time paid homage and tribute to Solomon. The queen of Sheba heard of the fame of Solomon and came to test him with questions, but Solomon was able to give an answer to all the questions. Jesus said of himself that He was greater than Solomon in wisdom. Jonah preached to the people of Nineveh. In one message, every person of the city repented and turned to the Lord from the king, even to the least of the people of the city. But Jesus said of himself, "Greater than Jonah is here." Are you willing to hear Him?

54. Jesus was warning the people of His day, and He is warning us today who we must fear. There are some heartless, cruel, and wicked rulers. In Moses's days, there were the Pharaohs who threw all the baby boys in the Nile River. In Jesus's days, King Herod killed all the boy babies (two years old and under) when he heard of the birth of Jesus, labelled the king of the Jews. In our recent history, Hitler of Germany killed six million Jews and countless others. However, these wicked men can only kill you and can do no more. But Jesus is able

to kill you and cast you into hell. Fear Jesus, and hear Him.

55. Getting ready is not ready. Almost ready? You are still not ready. Although you know the day, hour, and even minute your airplane, train, or bus is departing, sometimes you are still late. If you are lucky, sometimes they may wait for you. But no man knows the day, hour, or minute of Jesus's coming, and He won't be waiting for you when He comes. So you must be ready. Will you be ready?

56. Witchcraft can't help. And if you do it, it will cost you your soul. The cost for doctor's fees is high and often a long process. If the doctor can help and the process is not long, only some of us can afford the cost. When Jesus heals you, it costs you nothing, and the process is immediate. This is why you should glorify Jesus as Lord and Savior.

57. Which of the groups are you in? The nine of the ten or the one of the ten? Nine lepers did not find it worthy to return to give thanks to the healer. They went on their merry way, as if nothing was done unto them. One of the ten lepers who was healed saw that he was cleansed and turned back to glorify God. You may not be a leper, but is there something in your to give the Lord Jesus thanks for? Yes. The air we breathe, our eyes to see, our strength to walk, the food on our tables, and many other favors. I will say like in the Psalms, "I will bless the Lord at all times; His praises shall continually be in my mouth."

58. Oh, what a day. A glorious day for some and a sad and mournful day for others. When the Lord Jesus shall shine in the heavens on His day, when your eyes behold Him, what will you do?

59. A certain ruler came to Jesus and saluted Him as a good master. It is a hard thing for a ruler to call anyone whom he thinks is his subject good and, more so, master. He then went on to ask Jesus the most important question: "What shall I do to inherit eternal life?" Maybe all of us would accept the salutation of "Good Master" even if we were not good—more so, the title "master" even if we were servants. But Jesus, in His humility, wanted to know why the ruler was calling Him good. And Jesus declared to the ruler that there is none that is good, save one, and that is God. Is there anyone who could refrain himself from calling Jesus good? Jesus says He is the Good Shepherd. So then, if you know that Jesus is good, then you know that He is the Almighty God. Jesus is not only a good man; Jesus is the only true and living God.

60. It is said that there are about 4,200 different religious groups in the world today, and each one teaches differently from the other. The religious teachers of Jesus's time testified that they knew Jesus and that He taught rightly. They also knew that Jesus was not a respecter of persons. They also knew that there is only one God. Jesus also teaches that there is one way to God, and Jesus is the way. Jesus teaches that He is the way, the truth, and the life. I am so glad that Jesus is my teacher and my only way.

61. If you were set to have a day in court, certainly you would consider what to say to convince the judge that you are not guilty as charged. Have you ever had a case in court and when the day drew near for you to face the judge, you began to think and write down what you are going to say to convince the judge that you are not guilty? Jesus says we should not do so, for He will give

us a mouth and wisdom that our adversaries cannot resist. I'm so glad that Jesus is my advocate, my defense as well as my lawyer.

62. Men hate one another for personal reasons, for things they believe you say about them, or for things they believe you have done to them or to someone close to them. Hatred brings strife, even unto death. We who believe in Jesus will not be hated for wrongdoing. We will not be hated by one man but by all men and women who do not accept the name of Jesus. But Jesus assures us that not one hair of our head shall perish. Jesus is our God; we know that He can protect us from all evil.

63. What a great honor it is to have Jesus as your defense. Jesus knows that the enemy desires to have us and sift us as wheat, but Jesus has put a hedge around us. Jesus has put us in the secret place of His pavilion. He has put us out of the reach of the enemy, where we are safe from all harm. Only trust Jesus.

64. Some people glorified the Lord Jesus for the things they saw and heard of Him. The angels, wise men, and the shepherd worshipped and glorified Him at His birth. Some people glorified Jesus for the miracles they received by His hands, like turning water into wine, multiplying the fish and bread, and raising the dead. But the centurion glorified Jesus when he saw Jesus die on the cross. He confessed that Jesus is a righteous man. Are you glorifying Jesus? And for what?

65–

66. Was Jesus boasting or exalting himself when He declared to the disciples that all the scriptures, from Moses and the prophets to the Psalms, were about Him? Do you know that all the scriptures are about Him? Oh, yes! That's why we worship Him only.

67. There are some traditions that we must keep, and there are some traditions that we must let go of. The tradition of preaching and teaching baptism in Jesus's name must be upheld in every nation, as it was done at Jerusalem on Pentecost day, as Jesus requires. Are you holding the tradition of baptizing in Jesus's name as the apostles did? Yes or no?

68. Are you worshipping Jesus? Are you worshipping them whom you don't know? The Word of God says, "Thou shall worship the Lord thy God and Him only shalt thou serve."

69. Some people are remembered and honored for the things they have invented. The incandescent light bulb was invented by Thomas Edison, Joseph Swan, and Hiram Maxim. The first locomotive engine was invented by George Stephan in 1812, and the list goes on. But all things were created by Jesus, and without Him is not anything made that was made. Jesus is the author and maker of everything. How do you remember Jesus?

70. In the world, we have many different types of light. We have the stars, the sun, and the moon. We also have electric light. We have candles, lamps, and, the newest of all, solar lights. But Jesus is the true light. He is the light that lightens every man that cometh into the world. Is Jesus your light?

71. If I should see a lion, a serpent, or a bear coming my way, I would be fearful. When John the Baptist saw Jesus coming, he introduced Jesus as an innocent lamb that came into the world to do a special job that no man could do. Jesus came to take away the sins of the world. Jesus took away my sins. Will you allow Jesus to take away your sins?

72. What a big difference it makes to be baptized with the Holy Ghost. You can be baptized in water by any man, but only Jesus can baptize you with the Holy Ghost, for He is the Holy Ghost.

73. The name of Jesus is far above every name in heaven and on earth. At the name of Jesus, every knee shall bow. When the people saw the miracles that Jesus did, they believed on His name, for they saw the good of the Lord in the land of the living. I'd rather be on David's side; I don't have to see to believe in Jesus's name. Which side are you on? To believe to see or to see to believe?

74. Oh, what a mystery of godliness. Jesus was on earth, speaking to Nicodemus, but Jesus was declaring that He was in heaven. Let us read this passage prayerfully and earnestly to see the omnipresence of Jesus. Jesus said, "And no man has ascended into the heaven, but he that came down from heaven" (John 3:13). Do you agree that Jesus is the only one who ascended into heaven and is also the only one who came down from heaven? If you agree, let's go to the next statement of Jesus: "Even the Son of man which is in heaven." Do you believe that Jesus was on the earth and in the heavens at the same time? Yes or no?

75–

76. Lifting up a serpent is very dangerous for anyone to do. Lifting up Jesus is joy and peace. Lifting up Jesus is done by praising Him. When you praise Jesus, He will deliver you from all harm, from all dangers, and from hell where the wicked will be punished forever.

77–

78. Not every man who comes into the world makes an impact. Some men impact their countries; some impact their communities, schools, churches, and families.

Some men even make impacts across class and racial lines. But when Jesus came into the world, he came that through Him, all men might be saved. No matter who you are and whatever state you are in, Jesus came to save all. Our natural life is so short and full of sorrows and trouble. Our life span is only three score and ten years. But Jesus came so that we might have eternal life through Him.

79–

80. There was a businessman who sold trucks for a living. A customer, who did not look desirable, looked the dealer in his eyes and ordered two trucks. To his surprise, he was chased away by the owner. The man then walked to another truck dealer just a block away. He asked the dealer the same question and bought two new trucks, cash. The dealer then called his competitor, the dealer who had chased the buyer away, and told him of his best sale in years. He then told him who the customer was. To his surprise, it was the same man he'd chased away. He just didn't know who the customer was. Jesus said to the woman at the well, "If thou knewest the gift of God, and who it is that saith to thee, Give me drink; thou wouldest have asked him, and he would have given thee living water." Do you know who Jesus is? Have you ever asked of Him?

81. It is good to take the mask off sometimes. The woman at the well took Jesus for just another man because Jesus was wearing a mask of flesh. She was confused where the place of worship should be because the Jews wor-shiped in Jerusalem and the Samaritans worshiped in the mountains. She knew something about the coming of Christ because she said, "When Christ shall come, he will tell us all things." Jesus then openly declared to the

woman who He is by saying to her, "I that speaketh, I am He." Do you know who Jesus is? The mask is off so that we can clearly see that Jesus is the true and living God.

82. There are times you will hear of some person, place, or thing that will get your attention. But you will often not be satisfied until you have a personal experience with the person, place, or thing. The men of the city (where the woman at the well came from) said unto her, "Now we believe not because of thy saying, for we have heard Him for ourselves." Do you know Jesus? Know Jesus for yourself. He will change your life forever.

83. Is the Father and the Son the same? Jesus says that all men should honor the Son even as they honor the Father. Exodus 20:3 states, "Thou shalt have no other gods before me." And Isaiah 43:10–11 states, "Ye are my witnesses, saith the LORD, and my servant whom I have chosen: that ye may know and believe me, and understand that I am he: before me there was no God formed, neither shall there be after me. I, even I, am the LORD; and beside me there is no saviour." Should we give all honor to Jesus our savior? Yes or no?

84. "Sing them over again to me, wonderful words of life." In our natural lives, we are passed from life to death. But if we hear the words of Jesus and believe the Word of Jesus, when we die, we are passed from death to life. Oh, what a great crossover from death to life, just by believing in the Word of Jesus.

85. Have you been searching the scriptures? Do you believe in the scriptures? Do the scriptures lead you to Jesus? All scriptures testify of Jesus: His power, His mercy, His goodness, His majesty, His honor, His glory, and all His wonderful works. They also testify of His resurrection,

His ascension, and His wonderful promise to return to receive us unto Himself. Are you awaiting His coming? Yes or no?

86–

87. All over the world, there is hunger and starvation. In some countries, the government cannot provide enough bread (food) for the people in need. But Jesus declared that He is the bread that comes down from heaven to give his life for the world. Jesus says if we will come to Him, we will never hunger or thirst again. When your spiritual needs are met, your natural needs are covered.

88. This is the all-inclusive, powerful will of God unto all men. No matter your status in life, you are included. Whether you are rich or poor, learned or unlearned, Black or White, Jew or Gentile, you are in His will. This is the will of God to us that whosoever seeth the Son (Jesus) and believes in Him may have everlasting life. What a wonderful, all-inclusive gift of God to us, just to see Jesus.

89. The world around us is dying. The water, the air we breathe, the trees, the animals, and (most importantly) humans are dying. Jesus gives us assurance that He will give His life for the saving of the world. Because Jesus lives, we shall live also.

90. Why should I want to stay when others are leaving in great numbers? The greater portion of Jesus's disciples stopped following Him because they saw Him as a failure. A small portion of Jesus's disciples stayed with Him because they saw Him as a success. When Jesus asked the few disciples who stayed if they will also go, Simon Peter gave two unprecedented answers: "To whom shall we go? Thou hast the words of eternal life. And we believe and are sure that thou art that Christ, the Son

of the living God." Are you sure who Jesus is? Will you stay, or will you go?

91–

92. Jesus is my all in all. He is a friend in the time of weariness and a light when shadows fall. Jesus is the door, the Good Shepherd, the living water, and the living bread. Jesus is the way, He is the truth, and Jesus is the life. Most of all, Jesus is my savior.

93. Yes, Jesus made the world, the sea, and the land; He held them together with His mighty hand. The great and mighty hand of Jesus is the most secure hiding place one could ever find. None can ever pluck us out of His hand. Are you safe where you are hiding? If not, come and hide in Jesus.

94. Words are powerful and have great meaning. Words that we do not understand mean nothing to us. Do you truly understand the Word of Jesus? When Jesus says, "He that believeth in me, though he were dead, yet shall he live: and whosoever liveth and believeth in me shall never die," do you believe and understand these words?

95. It is unlikely for servants to be where their masters are. Household servants are the closest to their masters. Other servants come and go to work daily. Jesus, our master, promises us that where He is, we will be also. We will not only be with Jesus but also be honored by His Father. Follow, follow, I will follow Jesus. What will you do?

96–

97. If you use both hands equally, you are called ambidextrous. If you speak more than one language, you are considered bilingual. If you are the master of more than one profession, you are a multicareer individual. What shall we then say about Jesus who can do all things and

of whom nothing is too hard or impossible for? Ask Abraham, Isaac, and Jacob. Ask Moses and Joshua. Ask David and all Israel. Read Hebrews 11, and you will see that Jesus has done all things well.

98. Our spiritual and temporal success depends on how much we embrace Jesus as Lord and Savior. Psalm 1:3 describes our life with Jesus in this manner: "And he shall be like a tree planted by the rivers of waters that bring forth his fruit in his season. His leaf also shall not wither and whatsoever he doeth shall prosper." If we abide in Jesus, this is the assurance we have in Him.

99. We can compare apples with apples and oranges with oranges, but we cannot compare the Lord Jesus with any other. We cannot compare the love of Jesus with any other love. There are some people who would die for their country, family, and friends, but if they could escape death, they would. However, though Jesus could've escaped death, He willingly laid down His life for us. Jesus has proven His love to us through death.

100. You may have chosen many people for many different purposes in your life: presidents, prime ministers, teachers, sportsmen, doctors, lawyers, and the list goes on and on. But maybe no one has ever chosen you. Maybe some of those whom you have chosen have rejected you. But in your lowly estate, when all have rejected you, Jesus, the King of glory, has chosen and ordained you to be a royal priesthood. And most of all, he has chosen you to be a son of God.

101. Don't be called doubtful like Thomas. Don't wait until you see before you believe. The Word of God in Romans 10:17 says, "So then faith cometh by hearing, and hearing by the word of God," and Hebrews 11:6 says, "But without faith it is impossible to please Him: for he that

cometh to God must believe that he is, and that he is a rewarder of them that diligently seek Him." Are you doubtful like Thomas, who had to see to believe, or are you faithful like Abraham, who believed though he did not see?

102. The Bible, which is the Word of God, is made up of two parts: the Old Testament and the New Testament. There are sixty-six books in the Bible, thirty-nine books in the Old Testament, and twenty-seven in the New Testament. There are 1,189 chapters; 31,102 verses; and 783,137 words that make up the Bible, and all of it is about Jesus. If you believe in the written words, it will become the Living Word. And by believing, you might have eternal life through His name. Even if you can't read the word but you hear the word and believe it, it is still effective to save you.

ABOUT THE AUTHOR

Pastor Ivan Blake was born in Kingston, Jamaica. He was baptized in the Kings Chapel Church of Jesus at the age of twenty-nine by Pastor Roy Skyers. In 1984, Pastor Ivan Blake was elevated to a Deacon. In just four years, he was elevated to assistant pastor and, soon after, became a pastor of the Kings Chapel Church in the Parish of St. Ann.

Pastor Ivan Blake was inspired to write this book to help people come to the knowledge of who the Lord Jesus is and why they should serve Him only.